At this livestock auction in New Holland, Pa., Amish
and non-Amish intermingle. The straw hats of the Amish,
are handmade. The hatmakers dry the straw, braid
it, sew it together, and then shape the headgear.

BEVERLY
PUBLIC
LIBRARY

MEET
THE AMISH

THE PEOPLES OF NORTH AMERICA

Introduction by
DANIEL PATRICK MOYNIHAN
U.S. Senator

MEET
THE AMISH

Fred L. Israel
Professor of American History
City College of New York

CHELSEA HOUSE PUBLISHERS
New York New Haven Philadelphia

Editor: Linda Grossman
Associate Editor: Paula Edelson
Editorial Staff: Perry King, John Selfridge, Alma Rodriguez-Sokol
Art Director: Susan Lusk
Design: Deborah Daly
Layout: Laura Hough
Cover Design: Robin Peterson
Picture Research: Juliette Dickstein
Editorial Coordinator: Karyn Gullen Browne

Library of Congress Cataloging in Publication Data
Israel, Fred L.
   Meet the Amish.
   (The peoples of North America)
   Bibliography: p.
   Includes index.
   Summary: Presents a survey of the Amish, their history,
   beliefs, and customs.   1.   Amish—Juvenile literature.
   [1. Amish]   I. Title.   II. Series.
   E184.M45I87   1986   973'.088287   85–17516
   ISBN 0-87754-853-6

Chelsea House Publishers
Harold Steinberg, Chairman & Publisher
Susan Lusk, Vice President
A Division of Chelsea House Educational Communications, Inc.

Chelsea House Publishers

133 Christopher Street, New York, NY 10014

345 Whitney Avenue, New Haven, CT 06510

5014 West Chester Pike, Edgemont, PA 19028

Photos courtesy of Pennsylvania Dutch Visitors Bureau, AP/
Wide World Photos, *Amish Society,* (Johns Hopkins University
Press), The Bettmann Archive, Amish Historical Society, *A Gal-
lery of Amish Quilts,* (E. P. Dutton and Co., Inc.), UPI/Bettmann
Newsphotos

CONTENTS

Who Are We?
Daniel Patrick Moynihan   **vii**

Preface
Professsor Fred Israel   **1**

1   History of the Amish   **9**

2   Practices and Beliefs   **25**

3   The Home and the Farm   **37**

4   Education   **57**

5   The Amish Today   **69**

Further Reading   **77**

Index   **78**

FRED L. ISRAEL is Professor of American History at the City College of New York. He is the author of *Nevada's Key Pittman* and co-editor of *A History of American Presidential Elections* and *The Justices of the United States Supreme Court,* also published by Chelsea House.

DANIEL PATRICK MOYNIHAN has served as U.S. Senator from New York since 1977. From 1966 he has held a professorship at Harvard University. Before his election to the Senate, Moynihan served with distinction in several positions in the Kennedy administration, as ambassador to India (1973–75), and as U.S. representative to the United Nations (1975–76). His numerous, highly praised publications include *Beyond the Melting Pot* (co-author; 1963) and *Loyalties* (1984). He co-edited *Ethnicity: Theory and Experience* (1975).

WHO ARE WE?

Daniel Patrick Moynihan

The Charter of the United Nations begins: "We the peoples of the United Nations...." This is easily explained. The U.N. is an organization made up of independent countries with distinctive peoples. By contrast, the Constitution of the United States begins: "We the People of the United States...." This seems to refer to only one people. Yet this fine set of histories is called THE PEOPLES OF NORTH AMERICA. Could this refer simply to Americans and Canadians? Not at all. Our series is filled with titles of people who have countries of their own: Austrians, Irish, Italians, Portuguese. What, then, are we studying here? We are studying the different ethnic groups which make up the population of our two countries. As no two on earth (or in history) the populations of the United States and of Canada are made up of persons who have migrated from just about every known part of the world.

Everybody in North America (which is comprised primarily of the United States, Canada, and Mexico) is an immigrant or a descendant of immigrants, the people who migrated here. First came the Indians and Eskimo, thousands of years ago, crossing the Bering Strait from Asia. The ear-

UNITED STATES

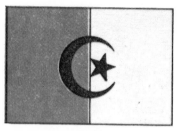

ALGERIA

AUSTRALIA

AUSTRIA

BELGIUM

BOLIVIA

liest Europeans were Vikings who never really established themselves here. It wasn't until the great age of exploration began, some five centuries ago, that European settlements began. From the start they were all mixed up as to nationality. Columbus, who explored the Caribbean in 1492, was an Italian in the service of the King and Queen of Spain. John Cabot, who first landed in Canada in 1497, was an Italian in the service of the King of England. (For that matter, Bering was a Danish captain in the service of the Czar of Russia.)

Hold a moment. What do we mean when we say that Columbus was an Italian? Would he have said that? Certainly not. There was no nation called Italy at that time, though there was an Italian language. Columbus, no doubt, thought of himself as a Genoese, from the city-state of Genoa where he was born. It is interesting to note that many of us think of ourselves as coming from countries that really didn't exist when our forebears actually arrived. Cabot, we said, sailed for the King of England. Scotland was a separate kingdom then, and would remain so for more than a century until the present United Kingdom was formed in the 17th century. Germany and Italy became nations in the 19th century. Poland, having disappeared in the 18th century, reappeared in the 20th. And so it has gone. Some countries were even founded here: the Republic of Czechoslavakia was proclaimed in Pittsburgh in 1918!

The idea that everybody belongs to a particular nation which deserves to be independent, with overriding claim to the loyalty of its citizens, is a relatively new idea and not necessarily a happy one.

Nationalism. It started with the French Revolution, became the dominant political force in Europe in the 19th century, and has since spread to the whole of the world owing to the decolon-

BRAZIL

ization principles of the United Nations. The great diplomat Talleyrand lived through the French Revolution, and afterwards observed the contrast: only those who had known the old regime could understand the *douceur de vivre,* the sweetness of life. The fierce nationalism of the 20th century has twice now nearly consumed the world in war. And this may be just the beginning of national-ism's destructive power.

BULGARIA

The United States and Canada are unique. Apart from the rather sparse population of Native Amer-icans, as we sometimes call the first immigrants, our peoples come from many different lands. The poet Robert Frost put it well. "The land was ours before we were the land's." Only slowly did the memories and manners of Europe, and Africa, and Asia recede from the newcomers. Yet this profusion of differences created a singularity.

CANADA

At a time in the world when religious and ethnic differences were becoming hugely impor-tant—from the religious wars in 17th-century Eu-rope between Catholics and various Protestants, to the 19th-century nationalist movements among Italians and Germans and Irish and Poles, to the near extermination under Nazi Germany of Jews and other racially or religiously defined groups in 20th-century Europe and the fierce religious and tribal collisions of newly independent Asia and Africa—*we* learned to live together.

CHILE

Scholars asked how it came about that the North Americans developed religious toleration. The answer is, we simply had no choice—there were just *too many* religions for any single one to dominate *all* the others.

PEOPLES REPUBLIC OF CHINA

Canada had an interesting and important ex-perience of this sort. Although in both world wars of the 20th century (1914–18 and 1939–45) Brit-ain and France fought together as allies, serious differences arose after World War II between French-speaking Quebec and the English-speak-

CUBA

CZECHOSLOVAKIA

DENMARK

DOMINICAN REPUBLIC

EL SALVADOR

FRANCE

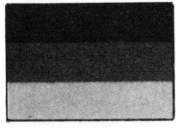

WEST GERMANY

ing provinces. Relations grew tense, then bitter, then violent. In 1963, on the advice of a French-speaking editor, an English-speaking prime minister established the Royal Commission on Bilingualism and Biculturalism, which Canadians came to refer to as the B 'n' B Commission. The assignment of the body was to study the growing crisis between "the two founding races" and propose measures to ease matters. Out of this came the important decision that the Canadian national government should be bilingual. All official documents and statements issuing from the capitol at Ottawa are now in both French and English. Bilingual education is greatly encouraged. Much good has come of these measures in terms of English-French accommodation. But those who were involved will tell you that another, somewhat unexpected element appeared which aided reconciliation. Commissioners travelling about Canada asked for advice on how to get the English and the French to live together as good neighbors. To their great surprise, just about everywhere they went they met Canadians, who were neither English *nor* French. They were Ukrainians, Germans, Italians, Chinese, Japanese, and, of course, many native Indian and Eskimo tribespeople. "Aren't we also Canadians?" they asked. And the answer was that of course they were. Slowly, or so it appeared to an American watching his northern neighbors, it dawned that there were all kinds of Canadians who cherished their ethnic and religious heritages and wished them preserved. What is more, there was *no* majority. Almost, but not quite, half the population came from the British Isles. But Scotsmen or Irishmen, or Welshmen hardly think of themselves as English! No, Canada, like the United States, is a land of immigrants for whom mutual tolerance is a matter of reason as well as principle.

Even as Canadians were unaware of their multiplicity, Americans were worried and even a

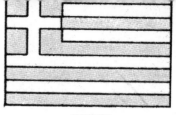

GREECE

HUNGARY

INDIA

IRAQ

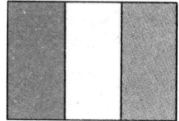

IRELAND

ISRAEL

little embarrassed by theirs. After Independence, the first great migration was that of the "famine Irish," driven here by the potato blight of the 1840s. Irish Catholics, they came in great numbers and settled in cities, enough to make the old settlers, mainly Protestants, nervous indeed. As the 19th century wore on, more and more immigrants arrived from Eastern and Southern Europe, as well as from Asia, and the fear and dislike of foreigners intensified. In 1882 Congress passed the Chinese Exclusion Act closing our doors, otherwise open freely to all, to this admirable people. Japanese were effectively excluded also.

In 1924 Congress passed our first immigration act, establishing quotas on a country-by-country basis, which discriminated against the "new" immigrants in favor of the old.

☆

In the meantime, the Civil War had been fought, the ordeal of the Union. There are many reasons the conflict broke out. It was, indeed, as the Southerners called it, a War Between the States. Constitutional issues about states' rights were surely involved. But the *cause* of the Civil War was slavery, the holding of black men, women and children in lifelong bondage as chattel property by their owners. Slavery is an ancient institution, and few civilizations have escaped it altogether. The Bible tells of the Jews as slaves in bondage in Egypt. But in the main, ancient civilizations thought of slaves as not particularly different from other people, only less fortunate. Typically, a slave was captured in battle; victory can go either way.

By mid-19th century, slavery in the United States was being defended as something more than just an economic institution. When the first African slaves arrived in the then-British colonies of the 17th century, their status was uncertain. There was no such institution in the mother country. On the other hand, Englishmen could rent

xi

ITALY

JAMAICA

JAPAN

MARSHALL ISLANDS

MEXICO

MOROCCO

themselves out, in a manner of speaking. Thousands on thousands of young men and women had come to the colonies as indentured servants. In return for their passage and keep, they agreed to work for a plantation owner or a craftsman or whomever for a fixed number of years, after which they would be free to do as they liked. A question arose in a Maryland court as to whether slaves were merely indentured for a period of service. The calamitous decree held that they were indeed slaves, bound to permanent servitude as were their children. This condition was wholly at odds with the beliefs and values which Americans generally held. After all, our Declaration of Independence states:

> We hold these Truths to be self-evident that all Men are created equal, that they are endowed by their Creator with certain inalienable Rights, that among these are Life, Liberty, and the Pursuit of Happiness . . .

In the end slavery had to go. Before it did, though, an essentially new idea began to gain currency that some peoples were different from, and inferior to, other peoples.

This belief gained unwarranted credibility from the publication in 1859 of the epic work of Charles Darwin, *On the Origin of Species by Means of Natural Selection, of the Preservation of Favoured Races in the Struggle for Life.* Darwin's work was entirely about animals and plants, but in vulgar or corrupt minds the doctrine of evolution—that man "descended" from the apes—took on entirely new meanings. It was asserted by some that different nationalities and races—note that Darwin's title includes that word—were at different stages of evolution, some "higher" than others. (The words "racism" and "racist" do not appear in English or French dic-

NETHERLANDS

NEW ZEALAND

NICARAGUA

NORWAY

PAKISTAN

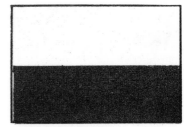

POLAND

tionaries until the 1930s.) Although in time these ugly ideas would be particularly directed against black people, they were by no means the first victims. The Irish were. As the 19th century went by, and the Irish multiplied in our cities, cartoonists, the "photographers" of the day, gradually changed the caricature of the typical "Paddy" from a recognizable North European to a near ape-like creature with jutting jaw and sloping forehead. The Chinese were depicted as a depraved and degenerate people, deficient in intelligence. Eastern European and Mediterranean peoples began to be distinguished by all manner of pseudo-scientific measures of physiogamy.

By the 20th century some of these doctrines had developed into virulent theories of a North European "master race." When Adolf Hitler came to power in Germany in 1933 the notion of "Aryan supremacy" became a state doctrine. "Aryan" refers to the Indo-European family of languages. Max Muller, the German-born scholar who traced the common roots of Sanskrit, Welsh, Russian and what you will once wrote that to speak of "an Aryan race, Aryan blood, Aryan eyes and hair" is as great a sin as to speak of a "dolichocephalic dictionary." (The dictionary in turn defines dolichocephalic as "possessing a relatively long head.") People got to be great skull measurers in the years after Darwin. If there was no limit to Hitler's ignorance, neither was there any limit to the evil he did. The German Nazi state from 1933–1945 set out to destroy the Jews of Europe, along with Gypsies and other "inferior" people and all but succeeded. Those within its reach were all but destroyed: gassed, burned, hung, starved.

It is necessary to remember the Holocaust if we are not to forget the horror that can come of unrestrained national, racial or religious attachments. G. K. Chesterton once wrote, "We are all ordinary men. Extraordinary men know this." He

xiii

PORTUGAL

ROMANIA

SAUDI ARABIA

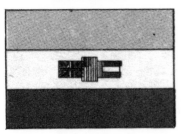

SOUTH AFRICA

SPAIN

SWEDEN

meant that what men and women have in common, across the widest range of region and culture, is so much more important than the differences among them.

But, say the French, *"Vive la difference!"* This was originally a reference to the ways in which women differ from men. But differences among peoples are also real, and can and should be celebrated. Every ethnic group has things that are special and important to it. And why not? Different histories, different accomplishments, different judgments, and of course different styles of dress and tastes in food linger long after the immigrant experience.

In our age, one of the most widely espoused political doctrines is communism, based on the work of Karl Marx, a German who published his first volume of *Das Kapital* in London in 1867. Of Marx's many predictions about the future, none was more central than the proposition that once nations became industrialized people would divide between classes of owners of capital, or productive wealth, and workers. The workers in turn would find that they had common interests with workers in other countries. Hence the slogan, "Workers of the World Unite!" How very wrong Marx was! Far from uniting in the years since he wrote it, the salience of ethnic, national and religious identity has become greater. Just look about the world today. What are people fighting each other about?

How supremely important it is then that *we* have learned to live with one another, respecting the ways in which we differ, while treasuring the things we share. In the United States, 1980 marked a kind of coming of age with regard to ethnicity. For the first time ever—in 190 years, that is—the decennial Census actually asked people about their ancestry. (The terms "ancestry group" and "ethnic group" were used inter-

xiv

TURKEY

U.S.S.R

UNITED KINGDOM

VENEZUELA

VIETNAM

YUGOSLAVIA

changeably.) To the surprise of many, a full 83% of the American people reported at least one specific ancestry; 31% provided a multiple response. Only 6% of the population reported they were simply "American."

The Census Bureau gave people a choice of more than 100 ancestry groups. (French Basque, Spanish Basque, Ruthenian, French-Canadian, Guamanian/Chamorro, British West Indian, Cape Verdean, Afro-American, Dominica Islander, Peruvian, Armenian, Chinese, Japanese to name just a few.) Our largest ancestry group was English, with 49.6 million. Together with the Irish (40.2 million), Scottish (10 million), and Welsh (1.7 million), we get just over 100 million persons from the British Isles, which is not far from the Canadian proportion but, again, not quite a majority. There is no majority! There were almost as many Germans (49.2 million) as English, but after the Irish (40.2 million) there is a big drop to the Afro-American (21 million). There are sizable French (13 million), and Italian (12 million) groups. Poles, Dutch, Swedes, Norwegians and Russians follow. But thereafter no group exceeds the 2 million mark. There is just that great and wondrous profusion, the aftermath of one of the greatest migrations in history, one that is hardly over as Koreans and Vietnamese and Nicaraguans and Cubans head for our shores.

It is important to know something of your own ancestry. It is yours after all, and is likely on closer examination to be rather different from the often-vague stereotypes and traditions you acquire while growing up. It is possibly even more important to know something of the ancestry of others you know or may get to know. In a sense they are part of your history too, for nothing so defines the American nation as the motto on the Great Seal, *E Pluribus Unum*—Out of Many, One.

Washington, D.C.
October, 1985

Three serious-faced Amish boys watch a farm sale near Strasburg, Pa. This particular auction raised money for the local fire company.

PREFACE

Within a few hours' drive from the heavily populated cities of the northeastern United States is an area of Pennsylvania where a group of people preserve a way of life entirely different from that of modern America. In southeastern Pennsylvania, primarily in the beautiful rural area of Lancaster and Berks counties, live the Amish people, who practice the customs and beliefs that have been passed down to them for almost 300 years.

CLOTHING

Present-day sightseers who see the Amish for the first time often feel as if they have stepped back into another century. The Amish regulate every facet of their existence according to their literal interpretation of the Bible. These people, who speak a dis-

Schoolboys peek out from under their straw hats on a sunny day. As Amish children grow up they often care for their younger siblings, helping them learn responsibility and persuading them to be obedient.

tinctive German dialect known as "Pennsylvania Dutch," wear clothing and maintain an unusual hairstyle prescribed by custom. The women and girls part their hair in the middle, and both sides are pulled tight around the back and rolled into a bun. They never cut their hair or curl it. Men and boys let their hair cover their ears and have long sideburns. Married men have beards, but single men are clean-shaven. Moustaches are forbidden.

Amish men wear black or dark blue jackets without lapels and loosely fitting pants held up by suspenders. No zippers, belts, or buttons are used; their clothing is held closed by hooks and eyes—a holdover from an earlier time in Europe when buttons were unknown. Neither jackets nor pants have pockets. Shirts are usually white, and no ties are worn. An Amish man is seldom seen without a hat—a broad-brimmed black felt hat or, in warm weather, a straw hat with a black band.

Amish women dress alike, wearing long, full-skirted dresses that nearly reach the ground. All the dresses are the same style, as if they were made from the same pattern. An apron is worn over the dress, with unmarried women wearing a white apron and married women either a black or darkly colored one. Only solid, somber colors are permitted—no plaids, stripes, checks, or bright colors are worn. This severely plain dress is devoid of any frill that might indicate worldly vanity. Amish women wear a white cap on the back of their heads with a bow under the chin. In colder weather the women wear heavy crocheted shawls, and the men use long black overcoats. Children are dressed in the same style as the adults. Almost all the clothing is made at home by the women. No one wears jewelry. The Amish have kept the same style of dress for centuries. Any divergence from the old styles is regarded with suspicion.

Who are these people who avoid the 20th century, who refuse to use electricity in their homes, own automobiles, radios, or television sets and do not go to the movies? Who are these people who adhere to a simple agricultural life, tilling the soil with horse-drawn plows, and who harvest their crops with sickles and scythes, leading an anachronistic lifestyle as they steadfastly reject the comforts and pleasures of modern technology?

An Amish couple take their two small children out for a ride in their horse and buggy. Differences in carriage structure, decoration, and harness vary from one Amish community to another and are subject to the rules (*Ordnung*) of each order.

POPULATION

They are people whose ancestors came to Pennsylvania, mainly from Germany and Switzerland, in the early part of the 18th century to escape persecution and to practice their religion, customs, and traditions as they believe were ordained by the Scriptures. Today, almost 25,000 baptized adult Amish live in 20 states and in the Canadian province of Ontario. The total Amish population has been estimated at three-and-a-half times the number of church members. But 75% reside in only three

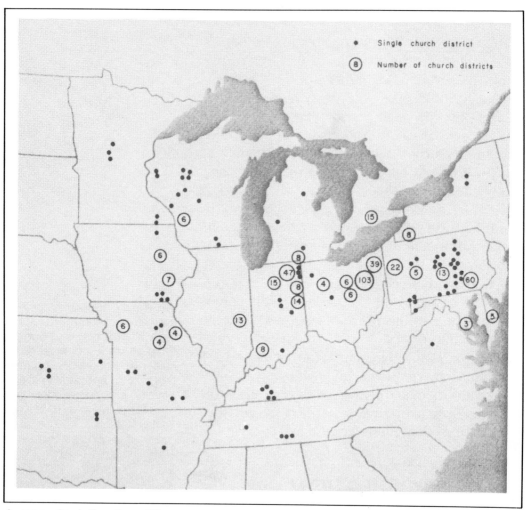

Single church district

(8) Number of church districts

A map depicting the different Amish settlements in North America.

states—Pennsylvania, Ohio, and Indiana—with the traditional seat being Lancaster County, Pennsylvania.

The Amish do not seek new members. They do not try to convert people. Very few outsiders have joined the group. Almost all are direct descendants of the first settlers. (In Lancaster County, five family names are held by more than 70% of the Amish population.)

Endogamy is practiced; that is, an Amish person must choose a mate from within the sect. Such a practice involves a great deal of intermarriage; hence almost all Amish are related to each other. In fact, the rate of inbreeding has created some genetic problems. The birthrate is high—seven or eight children per family is not uncommon, and about one-fifth of the families have ten or more children. All birth control methods are prohibited. Infant mortality is relatively low. Therefore, the number of Amish is increasing in spite of the temptations to assimilate into the world around them. One Amish man had 410 living descendants at the time of his death at age 95: five children, 61 grandchildren, 338 great-grandchildren, and six great-great-grandchildren. Their numbers have risen from less than 1,000 in 1800 to nearly 5,000 in 1900, and to approximately 80,000–90,000 today. This unique community is comparable to one huge extended family. It is this family structure that perpetuates Amish culture, faith, and traditions.

TOURISM

Ironically, the simple, unpretentious Amish way of life has spawned a major multimillion-dollar tourist industry. In fact, the Amish and their towns—with such strange names as Intercourse, Bird in Hand, Ronks, Fertility, Bareville, Goodville, Blue Ball, and Paradise—rank among the top ten tourist attractions of the United States. In 1984 alone, nearly five million people traveled through Lancaster County to view the Amish going about their daily tasks in an idyllic pastoral setting. Unlike reconstructed villages such as Jamestown, Va., Sturbridge, Mass., and Williamsburg, Va., where "townspeople" play a role, the Amish are a genuine community, with their well-kept farms, water wheels, covered bridges, one-room schools, and horse-drawn buggies.

A tourist bus speeds past an Amish buggy on a street in Lancaster County. The Lancaster County Amish were once the most trusted group among their peers in matters of religious orthodoxy. They are now regarded as lax by some western Amish communities for allowing even limited farm mechanization.

Unfortunately, commercialization by "outsiders" is rampant. Dozens of gift shops and motels now exist along the principal roads used by the Amish. Tourist literature abounds. One can visit a 71-acre "authentic" Amish homestead or watch as nine projectors with three screens answer on film: "Who are the Amish?" Buggy rides are offered that take the sightseers on a two-mile tour through the Amish area in an "authentic" Amish family carriage. There are restaurants that promise an authentic Amish meal and gift shops with souvenirs of every imaginable description, Amish-style bonnets, straw hats and quilts, crocheted booties, salt-and-pepper shakers shaped in the image of an Amish couple, and even figurine Amish candle holders. At the Amish Farm and House, hostesses describe an "authentic replica" of an Amish kitchen. For the more independent tourist, there is a 90-minute auto-tape tour on cassette. As a further example of commercial intrusion into their privacy, a feature film (*Witness*) concerning the Amish and shot in Lancaster County, was released in 1985.

Indeed, as millions of tourists visit their countryside, we can only wonder how these devout, pious people feel about being regarded as so many museum pieces. Perhaps it is their strong faith that sustains them, their belief that God has called them to a life of dedication and humility. This belief enables them to avoid the tourists as politely as possible, almost as if the tourists did not exist. Without this dedication, the Amish might have disappeared many decades ago.

A hitch of eight Belgian draft horses pulling a plow. These horses, descended from the Flemish great horse used in medieval battles, were brought to the United States in 1866. They are a popular horse among the Amish.

An Amish girl waits at the family buggy for her parents to return. Girls between the ages of four and six learn housekeeping and cooking skills while boys the same age begin to learn the basics of farming.

A farmer's market in Lancaster, Pa., provides farmers with the opportunity to sell directly to consumers. Such markets, common in Amish communities, help supplement family income.

CHAPTER ONE

HISTORY OF THE AMISH

For the 300 years of its existence, Amish culture has perpetuated the customs and religious beliefs of its founders with scarcely any variation. To comprehend their resistance to change, it is necessary to understand Amish religious history. This firmness of religious belief is carried over into every aspect of Amish culture. In fact, tradition is the cornerstone of their fellowship.

PROTESTANT REFORMATION

Amish history has its roots in the complex and far-reaching European Protestant Reformation of the 16th and 17th centuries. The Protestant Reformation, or Protestant Revolt, like the Renaissance, was a general reaction against medieval civilization. Although primarily a religious movement, the Protestant Ref-

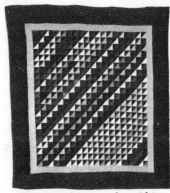

Diagonal Triangles, Ohio

Chapter openings show the brilliant varieties of textile folk art in these quilt patterns.

François Dubois, a Huguenot (Calvinist), painted this grisly scene of the St. Bartholomew's Day Massacre (1572), a slaughter of Protestants by Catholics that began in Paris on August 24 and spread throughout France. Within weeks 10,000 Huguenots had been killed. The Protestant leader, Admiral Coligny, was decapitated (right, center) and his head sent to Rome.

ormation profoundly affected the social, intellectual, and political life of Europe. Spiritually, the new Protestant religions challenged the Roman Catholic Church's claim to being the only religion through which individuals could achieve salvation. From the worldly point of view, the Reformation involved a struggle between the power of the all-embracing medieval Church and the rising national states. It was, in effect, a rebellion against the religious, political, and economic control wielded by the Catholic Church.

Martin Luther (1483–1546) was the leading figure in the opening phase of the Reformation. Originally, his purpose was to reform what he considered to be evils within the Catholic Church. Many in the Church, however, opposed Luther. Basically, Luther questioned certain practices within Catholicism that had become a standard part of the religion but, according to his reading of the Bible, were not practiced at the time of Christ. Several powerful German princes, who opposed the papal claims of universal authority, zealously supported Luther for their own political reasons. It was this support that gave the Reformation its impact and brought about the collapse of papal authority in a large part of Germany.

Above: Martin Luther posts his 95 Theses on the church door in Wittenberg, Germany. One practice he condemned was the Catholic policy of indulgence, which gave papal absolution for a sin in exchange for an act of penance. Penance could include participation in the Crusades; usually it was a financial contribution to the Church. Luther believed that penance could only be offered to God.

Left: Portrait of Martin Luther by the great Northern Renaissance artist Hans Holbein the Younger. Luther decided to become a monk after he was struck by lightning and survived. Later he became disenchanted with aspects of Roman Catholicism and led the Protestant Reformation.

11

THE SWISS REVOLT

A 16th-century portrait of Huldreich Zwingli, the great Reformation leader, who preached that anyone, even non-Christians, could enter heaven if they led decent lives. The Swiss leader's liberal views prompted Martin Luther to label him a heretic. Zwingli was killed during later Catholic-Protestant violence.

Independent of Luther, a similar reform movement started in Switzerland at almost the same time. Led by Huldreich Zwingli (1484–1531), the movement also aimed to correct alleged abuses within the Catholic Church. Zwingli derived much support for his own convictions from reading Luther's early pamphlets. Although he denied being a disciple of the German leader, many of Zwingli's ideas markedly resembled those of Luther.

From his pulpit in Zurich, Zwingli demanded immediate religious reform. In 1523, the Zurich city council held a series of debates. As the basis for his arguments, Zwingli prepared 67 statements, or theses, which contained the essence of his ideas. In them, he asserted the sole and absolute authority of the Bible and affirmed the doctrine of salvation by faith—that is, one can hope to have an eternal life based on faith alone.

Zwingli rejected many of the most fundamental tenets of Catholicism. He rejected the papacy, saints, fasts, pilgrimages, monastic orders, the priesthood, holy relics, indulgences, the sacraments of Mass, confession, and absolution, and the concept of purgatory. Many of his proposed reforms were even more extreme, more austere, than those of Luther.

Soon, under Zwingli's influence, the city of Zurich abolished the Mass. Religious statues, pictures, crucifixes, altars, and candles were removed from the churches. Relics were destroyed. Holy water was done away with, and even church frescoes were covered with whitewash. To Zwingli, since none of these practices could be found in the Bible, they were evil and detracted from the true spirit of Christian belief.

Zwingli's reforms were more thorough than those of Luther, but both men agreed on the basic doctrines of Protestantism. On one main point, however, they had a fundamental difference—on how to interpret the Last, or Lord's, Supper, the meal Jesus and his disciples had on the eve of his crucifixion. Belief in this event is fundamental to all Christians. Luther held that in the Eucharist (a rite commemorating Christ's sacrifice), "This is my body" must not be interpreted literally. His is the theory of *consubstantiation* (where the wafer and wine of the Eucharist do not become the body and blood of Christ, although after consecration, Christ's flesh and blood co-exist in the bread and wine) as contrasted with the Catholic belief in *transubstantiation*, where the bread and wine are considered to be literally transformed into the flesh and blood of Christ. Zwingli, on the other hand, regarded the bread and wine of the Eucharist only as symbols of the body and blood of Christ. In 1529 Luther and Zwingli engaged in a series of debates in Marburg, Germany, but their differences on the Eucharist proved irreconcilable. Luther refused to change his interpretation, which to Zwingli was but another relic of Catholicism. This profound disagreement on the fundamental Christian ceremony marked the first major division in Protestantism—and led to the creation of two new churches—Lutheran and Reformed.

Conflicts between Catholics and Protestants caused much of Europe to seethe in religious and political turmoil throughout most of the 16th and 17th centuries. And, almost from the beginning, there were dozens of splits among the Reformed (Zwingli) group. In 1525, also in Zurich, Konrad Grebel (c. 1498–1526) became the leader of a small group who questioned some of Zwingli's reforms, especially his emphasis on the baptism of infants, as opposed to baptizing adults who could declare their beliefs. Should the religious fellowship initiate in-

An Amish bookplate in an 1814 copy of the Mennonite prayer book, *The Martyr's Mirror*. This bookplate, executed in 1896, was decorated with Fraktur, a form of calligraphy used in Amish books since the late 1700s.

fants or mature believers? Should the fellowship be expansive or limited? Over this major issue of baptism, the Grebel followers, who came to be known as Anabaptists (a name given them by their opponents), broke with Zwingli. The true church, according to the Anabaptists, was to be composed of a voluntary group of disciplined adults and would not attempt to embrace the whole of humanity.

The Anabaptists, who would be severely persecuted for their beliefs, refused to baptize their children as ordered by the Zurich city council. They could not find a scriptural justification to support infant baptism. They would not accept any governmental authority over religious practices. Many historians credit the Anabaptists with being the first religious movement to preach total separation of church and state. This group, which separated from the Zwingli-controlled church, became known as the Swiss Brethren, or Mennonites, after Menno Simons (1496–1561), a Catholic priest who joined the Brethren in the early days and became one of its most influential leaders.

Zwingli led the persecutions against the Brethren, forcing them to flee Zurich. To the Brethren, or Mennonites, Luther and Zwingli were partial reformers. They sought to complete the work of these two men by attempting to interpret the Bible literally, without interference from any governmental authority. Their goal was to return to Christianity as it was practiced in the time of Christ. Because they accepted literally the Sermon on the Mount as the example for Christian behavior, the Brethren would not fight for or take an oath upholding any civil government. These ideas caused them to be branded as heretics by civil and ecclesiastical authorities.

The Mennonite book, *The Martyr's Mirror*, recounts the cruel tortures inflicted by both church and state on these early followers. To practice their religion as they understood it and to escape persecution, many Mennonites migrated to the New World, especially to Pennsylvania, a haven of religious freedom.

THE MENNONITE-AMISH SPLIT

The Mennonites, like so many other religious sects, experienced dissension over religious doctrine. In 1693, a Swiss Mennonite elder, who felt that his religion had lost its purity, broke with his church and formed a new religious sect. His name was Jakob Ammann (c. 1644–1730), and his followers are called Amish. The Mennonites and Amish, therefore, have common religious and historical roots.

Mennonites in 17th-century Europe. The family depicted in this drawing seems serene, showing no trace of the hardships that impelled them to emigrate to America.

The title page from the 1548 edition of a New Testament printed in Switzerland by the press of Christopher Froschauer. Many such Bibles were brought to America by Amish immigrants.

Perhaps the most important reason that the followers of Jakob Ammann separated from the Mennonites (1693–97) had to do with the practice of *meidung*, or the shunning, of excommunicated members. As Mennonites spread through Europe, differences developed over what to do with an adherent who violated the teachings of the religion and the sanctity of the fellowship. In some areas, wayward members were shunned at the communion table; in other areas, the errant ones were totally shunned not only in religious observances but in social and economic matters as well.

Jakob Ammann, who lived in the Swiss canton of Bern, believed that the general prevailing policy of shunning was not severe enough—that expelling a member from the communion was too lenient a punishment for those who had deviated from the religious fellowship. Ammann insisted that shunning must be total. He even demanded that the wife and children of an excommunicated member be prohibited from eating at the same table with the sinner, and that sexual relations should not occur between husband and wife until proper penitence had been made and restoration to the church obtained. He based this on the Biblical passage (1 Corinthians 5:11): "But now I have written unto you not to keep company, if any man that is called a brother be a fornicator, or covetous, or an idolator, or a railer, or a drunkard, or an extortioner, with such a one do not eat." Ammann also favored uniformity in dress and hairstyle. This aggressive leader began holding communion services twice instead of once each year, and he introduced the practice of footwashing, a reenactment of the biblical account of Jesus washing the disciples' feet (John 13), a rite also observed twice a year.

The followers of Ammann, who equated strictness with divine sanction, and those who did not accept his literal Biblical injunctions as the basis for every aspect of life, could not resolve their differences. Ammann's supporters split with the Mennonites to form a new religious sect—the Amish. It is estimated that of the 69 Swiss and German ministers involved in this theological debate concerning the purity of the religion, 27 sided with Ammann. Reconciliation efforts failed, and a new sectarian movement began.

Even before this bitter split, some Mennonites

had settled in Pennsylvania to escape persecution. The first permanent Mennonite settlement in the New World was in Germantown, Pa., in 1683, after the purchase of some 5,000 acres from the colony's founder, William Penn (1644–1718). The Amish began to arrive in the early 1700s. Today, there are no Amish in Europe. It is only in North America that the distinctive practices of their religion have survived.

Although much of the bitterness between the Mennonites and the Amish has subsided and these two Anabaptist groups have lived as neighbors for almost 300 years, the divisions still persist despite their common religious and historical roots. The main issue dividing them has almost always concerned lifestyle rather than basic Christian doctrine. In general, the Amish tend to be more conservative. They avoid modern technology. Most Amish, for example, use horse-drawn carriages, dress plainly, do not use electricity, and stress occupations involving the farm and home. Emphasis is placed on the local fellowship group. The Amish also forbid higher education for their members. Mennonites, on the other hand, are more accepting of education and 20th-century science and technology. Mennonites also support worldwide missionary activities as a way of enlarging the fellowship. The fundamental issue, now and in the past, has been the purity of religious practice.

IMMIGRATION TO THE NEW WORLD

For the Amish and other religious dissenters, Pennsylvania was unique. In Europe they were persecuted; in Pennsylvania they were free to practice their religion. Indeed, the idea of religious freedom

This portrait of William Penn, who founded Pennsylvania in 1682, was painted about 1666. Around that time Penn's conversion to Quakerism, begun when he was at Oxford, became complete. His father beat him for his Quaker beliefs. Penn was sentenced to the Tower of London after he wrote *The Sandy Foundation*, a strong attack on Anglicanism.

was a radical one for the times. William Penn, who had been jailed and harassed in England for his Quaker beliefs, clearly understood that individual freedom had to include freedom from government imposition of any religious doctrine on its citizens. He founded Pennsylvania with a specific pledge of religious liberty for all.

A full century before the adoption of the Constitution and the Bill of Rights, Penn saw the need for, and implemented, guarantees of absolute religious freedom. Pennsylvania became a refuge for numerous and diverse religious groups—including the Amish, Mennonites, German Baptist Brethren (Dunkers), the Schwenkfelders, Moravians, Catholics, and Jews—who had encountered persecution elsewhere. (The spirit of religious freedom that pre-

A love feast among the Dunkers, a sect similar to the Mennonites, as depicted by Howard Pyle. The Dunkers, many of whom migrated to America from Germany in the early 18th century, practice footwashing, the laying on of hands, annointing with oil, and use the kiss of charity. Their name refers to their baptism rite of immersion.

vailed in Pennsylvania also stimulated religious thinking, and several religious denominations originated in the state, including the Seventh-Day Adventists, the United Brethren, and the Disciples of Christ.) The largest concentration of Amish is still in Pennsylvania, particularly in Lancaster County, where the descendants of those early Amish settlers practice their religious beliefs as their forefathers did when they arrived in Penn's colony.

From the beginning of their settlement in Pennsylvania, the Amish displayed a high degree of mobility. Always searching for cheaper and more remote land, settlers moved into Delaware, Maryland, Ohio, and Illinois. By the early 1840s, they were among the first settlers in the Iowa Territory.

ARRIVAL IN CANADA

For several Amish families, even Pennsylvania of the 18th century was too strife-ridden. The American Revolution reminded them of the wars in Europe and of the persecution that their ancestors had endured because of their pacifist views. Even though the Continental Congress granted the Amish community exemption from military service during the American Revolution, several families began the trek on foot or by Conestoga wagon to the remote territory then known as Upper Canada. After having lost all their possessions en route, the first Amish group arrived at the Niagara River in 1776. At that time Canada did not have a central government with sufficient authority to issue land grants, so the newly arrived Amish became squatters in the territory. They chose to settle on land covered with black walnut trees because these trees grow in limestone soil, the kind best suited for farming. Thus, Essex

An Amish family drives a mule-drawn wagon loaded with all their household possessions. An airplane in the background provides a sharp contrast in transportation between the Amish and their neighbors.

A sleigh is used during winter to take children to and from school. Amish children once attended public schools, but have recently built their own one-room schoolhouses such as this one.

and Kent counties in southeastern Ontario have had Amish settlers since 1778.

In about 1796, the governor general of Canada advertised the availability of Canadian lands in Pennsylvania newspapers, and another small group of Amish emigrants made their way to Ontario. They brought healthy cattle, sturdy furniture, and funds to buy good land. Much of the agricultural pattern in Ontario began with these early Pennsylvania emigrés—such features as the family farm, the log house, and the bank barn.

Today, Elmira in Waterloo County, approximately 75 miles west of Toronto, is the leading Amish settlement in Canada. The Amish first settled here in 1800, and they now number about 1,000. Their self-sufficient community is as strongly opposed to outside influences as their counterparts in Lancaster County. While horses and buggies can be seen in Elmira, the Amish here live in areas more remote from paved roads and cities. Therefore, the Ontario community is not as exposed to the inroads of tourism and commercialization. As in Pennsylvania, the Waterloo Amish do not encourage their children to continue education beyond the eighth grade because they fear any higher education will expose their children to temptation and worldliness. These Waterloo Amish follow the same religious practices and have the same style of dress as do their Pennsylvania brethren.

A covered bridge. These wooden constructions, quite common in the 19th century, were inexpensive to build. Many have decayed, however, and the covered bridge is now a rare sight in America. But the Amish continue to maintain them.

Young children peep out the rear of their buggy. Parents encourage their sons and daughters to express their emotions freely, but do not allow sulking or self-pity.

CHAPTER TWO

PRACTICES AND BELIEFS

Religion is central to Amish culture. For these people, life has no purpose apart from service to God. The Amish adhere to a Christian faith in which the Scriptures dictate every aspect of life. Thus, the Bible is not only a religious text, but a strict guide to everyday living as well.

The Amish do not believe in formal church buildings. They meet in various homes for Sunday services, which are held every other week. The place of meeting is rotated, usually on an annual basis. Church membership consists of adults who have voluntarily committed themselves to the fellowship and to the discipline of their fellow believers. Amish settlements are divided into districts, and each district consists of about 75 baptized members. If the district becomes much larger, it is again divided. Visiting the services of other districts is encouraged, and the great intermingling of the Amish diminishes any formal barriers among districts.

Baskets, Pennsylvania

Buggies lining an Amish farm lane on a Sunday morning in Lancaster County indicate that an Old Order Amish worship service is about to begin. The Amish "meetings" take place in the homes of members. Note the traffic signs on the buggies.

In the religious hierarchy, there are bishops, ministers, and deacons. The bishop, the chief religious figure, can serve several districts. He performs marriages, baptisms, admits new members, and supervises the moral behavior of his flock. If there is any disciplinary action to be taken against a member, it is the bishop who determines the punishment. The ministers conduct the Sunday services and deliver sermons. The deacons handle administrative and financial matters affecting the district, and also assist poor members. Donations are accepted twice a year, and there are no collections at a service.

No formal training or apprenticeship is required for church officials. No special ceremony of ordination takes place. On the contrary, ministers and deacons are chosen from the men of the district by drawing lots. When an office is to be filled, can-

Joan.18.
d

† Der Han wirdt nit krähen, biß du mich drey mal haſt verlöugnet.

Das XIV. Cap.

Ein ſchöne predig in deren er ſeine jünger ver=
manet zů leyden und gedult, zů demůt,
glauben, und liebe. Er verheiſt auch inen
den geyſt.

A

Nd er ſprach zů ſeinen jüngern: Euwer hertz erſchräcke nitt. Glaubend jr in Gott, ſo glaubend auch in mich. In meines vatters hauß ſind vil wonungen. Wo aber das nit wäre, ſo hette ich es euch geſagt: Ich gon hin euch wonung zebereyten. Und ob ich hin gang euch die ſtatt zebereyten, wil ich doch wider kommen, und euch zů mir nemmen, auff das

Joan.8. b

jr ſygind wo ich bin. † Und wo ich hin gon, das wüſſend jr, und den wäg wüſſend jr auch.

Spricht zů im Thomas: Herr, wir wüſſend nit wo du hin gaaſt, und wie mögend wir den wäg wüſſen?

Joan.1. a
11. c
*Joan.6.c

Jeſus ſpricht zů im: Ich bin der wäg und die warheyt und das † läben. * Niemants kumpt zum vatter dann durch mich. Wenn jr mich kanntind, ſo kanntind jr auch meinen vatter. Und von nun an kennend jr jn, und habend jn geſehen. Spricht zů im Philippus: Herr, zeig uns den vatter, ſo benügt uns. Jeſus ſpricht zů im: So lang bin ich by euch, und du haſt mich nit erkennt? Philippe, wär mich geſehen hat, der hat den vatter geſehen. Und wie ſprichſt du dann,

Joan.10.
c

Zeig uns den vatter? † Glaubſt du nit das ich im vatter, und der vatter

*Joan.3.c
7. b 8. c
12. f 14. c

in mir iſt? * Die wort die ich zů euch red die red ich nit von mir ſelbs: der vatter aber der in mir wonet, der ſelb thůt die werck. Glaubend mir das ich im vatter, und der vatter in mir iſt: wo nit, ſo glaubend mir doch

B

umb der wercken willen. Warlich warlich ich ſag euch: Wär in mich glaubt der wirt die werck auch thůn die ich thůn, und wirdt gröſſere dann diſe

Matt.21.c
Mar.11. c
Joan. 15.
a 16. c

thůn: dann ich gon zum vatter. † Und ſo jr etwas werdend den vatter in meinem Nammen bitten, das wil ich thůn, auff das der vatter gepreyſet werde in dem ſun. So jr etwas bittend in meinem Nammen, das wil ich thůn.

Liebend jr mich, ſo haltend meine gebott. Und ich wil den vatter bitten, und er ſol euch einen anderen tröſter geben, das er bey euch bleybe ewiglich [namlich] den geyſt der warheyt, welchen die welt nit mag empfahen, dann ſy ſicht jn nit, und kennet jn nit: jr aber kennend jn, dann er bleybt by euch, und wirdt in euch ſein. † Ich wil euch nit weyſen laſſen, ich komme zů euch. Es iſt

Pſal.45. a
Matt.28.c

noch umb ein kleine zeyt ſo wirdt mich die welt nit mer ſehen, † jr aber ſöllend mich ſehen: dann ich läb, und jr ſöllend auch läben.1. An dem ſelbigen tag werdend jr erkennen das ich im vatter

Joan. 20.
b c d 21. ab

bin, und jr in mir, und ich in euch. † Wär meine gebott hat, und haltet ſy, der iſts der mich liebet: wär mich aber liebet, der wirdt von meinem vatter geliebet

Joan. 15.
a
1.Joan.5.
a

werden: und ich wird jn lieben, und mich ſelbs jm offenbaren. Spricht zů im † Judas, nit der Iſcariotes: Herr, was iſts dann, das du uns wilt dich offenbaren, und nit der welt? Jeſus

Acto.15. c

antwortet, und ſprach zů im: Wär mich liebet, der wirt mein wort halten, und mein vatter wirt jn lieben: und wir werdend zů im kommen, und wonung bey jm machen. Wär aber mich nit liebet, der haltet min wort

C

nit. † Und das wort das jr hörend,

Joan. 3. e
7. b 8. c 12. f
14. a

iſt nit mein, ſonder des vatters der mich geſendt hat.

Sölichs hab ich euch geſagt, dieweyl ich bey euch gweſen bin. Aber der tröſter der heilig geiſt, † welchen

Acto. 2. a
2.Tim.1.a

mein vatter ſenden wirt in meinem Nammen, *der ſelbig wirt euch alles

*Joan.16.
b

leeren, und euch erinneren alles deß das ich euch geſagt hab.

Den friden laß ich euch, meinen friden gib ich euch: nit gib ich üch wie die welt gibt. Euwer hertz erſchräcke nit, und förchte ſich nit. Jr habend gehört das ich euch geſagt hab: Ich gon hin, und kumm wider zů euch. Hettend jr mich lieb, ſo wurdend jr euch fröuwen das ich geſagt hab, Ich gon zum vatter: dann der vatter iſt gröſſer dann ich. † Und nun hab

Joan. 13.
b 16. a

ichs euch geſagt, ee dann es geſchicht, uff das wenn es nun geſchehen wirt, das jr glaubind. Ich wird hinfür nit vil mit euch reden, Dann es kumpt der † fürſt diſer welt und hat nichts

Joan. 12.

an mir. Aber uff das die welt erken=

p   ne

A page from the 1744 edition of a 16th-century Swiss New Testament printed in Fraktur, a heavy, black-letter typeface favored by early German printers and still used by the Amish.

didates are suggested by other church officers and by members of the district. At a Sunday service, those nominated are called to the front of the room, where there are as many Bibles as candidates. Each is instructed to turn to a given text. The one who finds a slip of paper at that page is the new official. The bishop is chosen by lot from among the ministers. Each district has a bishop, two ministers, and a deacon. The Amish believe that selecting church officials by lot enables God to choose the best man.

SUNDAY MEETINGS

According to tradition, men and women are separated at these Sunday services. If there is not enough space in one room, the single members are placed in other rooms, where they are also separated by sex. When the service begins at about 8:30 AM, with all seated on wooden benches, the men remove their hats. Hymn singing opens the service, but musical instruments are forbidden. The tunes have been passed down for generations, as the hymn books have only the words.

The Amish use the *Ausbund* hymnal, which consists of about 50 hymns. It is the oldest Protestant hymnal in use in America. The first edition was printed in 1564 by Anabaptists in Germany. Although Mennonites no longer use these hymns, they are still sung by the Amish. Basically, they are tales of the suffering, humiliation, and torture endured by the ancestors of the Amish. The hymns describe the sorrow of a people who tried to protest against the wickedness of this world and tell of those who attempted to crush their righteousness. Instead of being melancholy, the hymns speak of conviction, of courage, and of the assurance that God will not forsake his own but will lead them through sorrow

to an everlasting life. There is no particular order in which the hymns are sung. An elder will call out a hymn, set the pitch, and the congregation will follow. The "Hymn of Praise" is the one most often sung. Other, more sprightly, hymns are reserved for special occasions, such as weddings.

After the singing a sermon in High German follows, lasting about 30 minutes. The minister who is to preach is chosen by other ministers present on the day of the service. Sermons are extemporaneous. It is believed that in this way the word of the Lord will come through. Silent devotion follows. Next, the deacon reads from the Bible, followed by another minister's longer sermon, also in High German. (The Amish use a Bible printed from old metal plates, which they own and lend to a local printer.) Subsequently, the congregation hears personal testimonials. The service ends with a benediction. An

Amish *Ausbunds* (hymnals) printed in 1767 and 1801. Many of the lyrics of Old Order Amish hymns are quite gruesome, most having been written by 16th-century martyrs awaiting their death sentence. The music is based on Gregorian chants, folk tunes, and other melodies.

average Sunday service lasts about three hours. There is little variety in format. Emphasis is on the past — past suffering, past hardships, and past martyrs.

Following Sunday church services, a meal is served. The bishop, ministers, and deacons eat first, followed, in order, by older married men, younger married men, women, and, finally, the children. Men and women eat separately. When one is finished eating, the dishes are passed to the next without washing them but merely wiped clean with a piece of bread. The meal is practically standardized to avoid competition among the host families— bread, jellies, pickles, cheese, coffee, and fruit pies are served. Everyone is expected to remain for this meal, which is also a grand social occasion. The rest of Sunday is reserved for visiting relatives.

The Amish children perform Christmas carols for their mothers in a one-room school near Kalona, Iowa. Married women wear traditional white hats, or *Kapps* and unmarried women wear black hats for services, white hats at home.

RITES AND CEREMONIES

Communion is one of the most important parts of Amish religious activity. It is held twice a year, in the spring and the fall. The communion service is considered a demonstration of the unity of the religious community and shows that no major rifts or divisions exist among the membership. Approximately two weeks prior to the ceremony, a one-day service of self-examination is held. All church members are usually present. The bishops and ministers state the church rules. Each member is then asked if he or she agrees with the rules and is at peace with the other members. The service itself is simple, but it is the most revered of all the ceremonies. The preachers pass pieces of homemade bread and a large cup filled with wine to each communicant. In High German, the words "This do in remembrance of Me . . ." are intoned.

Following communion, the ceremony of footwashing occurs. The members are divided by sex. The men and women then form pairs and wash each other's feet. This ritual is followed by the exchange of the "holy kiss" between the pair (2 Corinthians 13:12). The footwashing reflects the humility of the members and also symbolizes the washing and purification of the soul in the blood of Christ (John 13:4–17).

Baptism is held before the second of the semi-annual communion services in the fall. At that time, new members are initiated into the fellowship. Like the Anabaptists, the Amish believe that baptism is an act that demands a total personal commitment, and they refuse to baptize infants. New members are generally over 16. Young Amish usually begin to take instruction in Bible study and church rules approximately four months prior to their baptism. It is performed by the bishop, who pours water over the heads of the new members. The young people are given an opportunity to change their minds and are told that it is better not to take the vow than to do so and later break it. It is estimated that about 85–90% of the young adults join the church of their parents. Once a young person is baptized, he or she is a full church member. In reality, though, while the Amish do provide a period of formal instruction prior to baptism, Amish families have spent many years in preparing their children for this special day. Of those baptized the percentage who eventually leave the church is extremely small.

MARRIAGE

When a couple wants to marry, the prospective bridegroom notifies the deacon, who confidentially inquires if the bride's parents approve. Rarely, if ever, does an Amish marriage occur without parental approval. If nothing stands in the way, the bishop announces the planned marriage about two Sundays before the formal vows. Engagements are not festive or romantic. Young couples meet at church services and holiday songfests. All relatives and friends are invited to the wedding, which is an elaborate social affair.

The marriage service itself takes place either on a Tuesday or a Thursday, traditionally in November after the harvest. The bishop presides. Gowns and tuxedos are forbidden. There are no kisses, rings, photographers, florists, or caterers. The groom wears his Sunday clothing, and the bride, for the first and only time in her life, wears a white garment. After the simple ceremony, a day of feasting and singing follows. The bride and groom spend their wedding night at the bride's home. There is no honeymoon. In fact, the couple do not live to-

Amish buggies are a common sight on many of the country roads of Lancaster County. Because of their religious beliefs, Old Order Amish residents of the area depend on the horse and buggy rather than cars for transportation.

In 1957, this Amish man registered to serve jury duty on a murder trial where the accused allegedly killed an Amish farmer in Ohio. The juror faced a moral conflict because the prosecutor asked for the death penalty, but Amish belief does not hold with capital punishment.

gether until the following spring after a rather ritualistic period of weekend visits with family and friends.

Parents assume responsibility for the new couple's farm. Family and friends provide furniture, quilts, rolls of linoleum, home-canned foods, farm tools, and the other basic necessities needed by the newlyweds. The new couple always receives a great deal of support from parents and friends. Marriages

last a lifetime because divorce is unthinkable in Amish society. Desertion and separation are practically unknown. The Amish frequently remarry after the death of a spouse. Out of respect for the deceased, however, the widow or widower does not usually remarry until at least a year has passed. The ceremony for a second wedding is even more simple than for the first.

"DUST TO DUST..."

The Amish maintain simple burial and funeral rites. Some Amish communities embalm the bodies but most do not. The deceased is prepared for burial by family and friends. The tasks of informing relatives, preparing the burial site, and constructing the plain pine coffin, are carried out by relatives and neighbors. The immediate family is relieved of all farming and domestic responsibilities as others take over these tasks. No payment of any kind would ever be considered for this assistance.

The funeral is usually held three days after the death. Amish funerals are large affairs, with relatives and friends often coming from long distances to attend. There is a sermon but no eulogy. Instead, the bishop or ministers stress the fact that the Bible admonishes everyone to be ready for death. The young are reminded that death is inevitable and that one should live so as to be prepared for it. Every Amish community has a small cemetery; usually a corner of a field is fenced off for that purpose. There are no family plots. The concrete headstones on the tombs record only the name of the deceased and the dates of birth and death. The Amish regard life as a means to "store up treasures in heaven," and death is looked upon as a natural part of the life cycle, when one's reward is realized.

A young Amish boy with his father during a sale of household goods and antiques in Ohio. Amish parents are loving but firm with their children.

CHAPTER THREE

THE HOME AND THE FARM

The Amish countryside of Lancaster County forms one of the most picturesque rural scenes in America. The bucolic setting, with its charming country lanes and roads, is pastoral life at its best. A sense of peacefulness and tranquillity prevails over the area.

The spacious farmhouse is the center of Amish life. There, babies are born and church services are held, as are weddings and funerals. The windows have shades but no curtains or blinds. No pictures or mirrors hang on the walls. There are no musical instruments of any kind. But colored, braided rugs, pillows, quilts, and spreads are everywhere. Hand-wound wooden gingerbread clocks are on the mantels. The simple furniture and chests are often decorated with old Pennsylvania Dutch designs. An indescribable beauty and charm permeate the stark simplicity.

Log Cabin, Barn Raising design, Ohio

All furniture is handmade. Boys learn carpentry at an early age and assist in making and repairing household articles. Amish women make most of the clothing for the families, as well as the lovely quilts. Although there are numerous "Amish quilts" offered for sale in the Lancaster area, few are authentic as the genuine ones are considered family heirlooms and are passed down. The farms and handmade furniture are also handed down from generation to generation and are seldom sold.

Many Amish homes, which have no electricity or telephones, are comprised of several houses that have been built onto the original structure. In these separate but attached sections parents live in one building and grandparents in another. Thus, two or three generations generally live under the same roof. In contrast to industrial societies where care of the elderly has become a major problem, the Amish extended family system eliminates the need for nursing homes for the elderly. Older people do not retire but rather withdraw gradually from farm work, at which time the younger family members take over the farm chores and move into the main house.

The three-generation house is a distinctive characteristic of the Amish. One of the dwelling units is the "grandfather" house, where the older couple moves when they retire, leaving the main responsibility of house and farm to the younger couple. Also pictured is a windmill, which the Amish use instead of electric power to draw water.

The Amish rarely accept any social security, medicare, or welfare payments from the government. If necessary, they will pay for but will not accept any type of government service. Because the elderly are cared for by their own, Congress, in a special ruling, exempted self-employed Amish from paying the Social Security tax. Medical services, if needed, are provided by local hospitals, but home remedies, rather than pills and other synthetically made medicines, are stressed. Good food, tea and vinegar, and homemade herb preparations are the standard medicines. No psychiatrists or analysts are ever consulted. Above all, it is the family and friends who nurture and care for the sick and elderly. Mutual aid, from birth to death, is at the center of Amish health care.

CUISINE

The large kitchen is the center of activity and the most important part of the house. Lighting is by kerosene or gasoline lamps. A wood- or coal-burning stove is used for cooking and heating. There is no plumbing, and water must be brought in from outside for cooking, drinking, and bathing. Perishable food is kept in the springhouse. In the kitchen, Amish men read the Bible, children play games, and the women cook. There are no modern utensils that depend on electricity. Amish dishes are prepared here: sausages of every type, bacon, sauerkraut, chicken-corn soup, chow-chow (spicy relishes), apple butter, jams and jellies of every description, and, of course, the wonderful pies and cakes for which Amish cooking is famous. Every meal ends with a fruit pie—apple, peach, cherry, rhubarb, apricot, or the well-known shoo-fly pie. Some Amish women bake pies to be sold at local markets. Fortunate is

WET BOTTOM PENNSYLVANIA DUTCH
SHOO-FLY PIE

Syrup Filling:

1 cup molasses—dark
1 cup hot water 1 level tsp. soda
dissolved in the boiling water
3 eggs
Stir and let cool

Crumb Topping:

4 cups flour
1 cup brown sugar
½ tsp. mixed spices: salt, nutmeg, ginger,
cloves, cinnamon, mace
½ cup shortening (no butter)
Combine ingredients to form crumb
mixture for pie topping.

Have two 9-inch unbaked pie shells ready. Pour syrup filling in crusts, dividing portions equally. Sprinkle crumb topping over syrup mixture, dividing topping equally between the two shells. Leave a little "air" in the center of the pies to allow for expansion and to prevent mixture from "boiling over." Bake 1 hour to 1 hour-10 minutes in 350 to 375 degree oven.

A recipe for one of the most traditional Amish dishes, shoo-fly pie. Tourists often go to farmer's markets in Lancaster County to buy this special treat.

the tourist who is able to purchase these delicious baked goods.

Every family preserves quarts of cherries, peaches, pears, and other fruits and vegetables. Almost every household makes its own cider, root beer, and ginger ale. Certain Amish-style restaurants in the Lancaster area, although not owned by the Amish, have attempted to recreate faithfully the simple cuisine of these people. In some, the menus are posted a week in advance. It is not unusual for the "locals" to plan their day's schedule around a good "Dutch" meal.

SOCIAL LIFE

Visiting is the most important social activity for the Amish, adding to the strong family and community cohesion and solidarity. A major social event for the young unmarried Amish are "singings," which are held almost every Sunday evening, often at the same place the church services were held. Church hymns are sung and refreshments are served. Local public sales or auctions provide occasions for more social activity. Few Amish in the area will miss an auction, which often takes on the atmosphere of a small fair, with men and women gathering in separate groups, talking and chatting.

Amish boys dressed up for Sunday service. During the time between adolescence and marriage, teenagers must decide whether they want to become baptized and join the Amish church.

RELIGION AND THE LAND

"To every thing there is a season, and a time to every purpose under the heaven: a time to be born, and a time to die; a time to plant, and a time to pluck up that which is planted. . ." (Ecclesiastes). Following Biblical injunctions, the Amish feel it is their responsibility to till the soil and bring forth an abundant harvest. They believe that farmers live especially close to God and nature, and nearly all are farmers. They consider the cities, like Sodom and Gomorrah, to be sinful and corrupt. In Lancaster County, more than 90% of the Amish cultivate the soil or are involved in such craft-related trades as harnessmaking, blacksmithing, and carpentry. Only a small number work away from the home. Some women, for example, make candy or hand-dipped candles in local shops or cook and bake in local restaurants. (A small group of Amish own a publishing house in Aylmer, Ontario, which publishes monthly inspirational magazines, texts for Amish schools, and historical books in High German.)

Their religious convictions also affect their farming methods. Farming is done without modern machinery. They use no tractors, electric pumps, or mechanical milking machines. Whatever is natural is ordained by God, not automation. The Amish farm, averaging from about 80 to 100 acres, is a family farm. Work is done by both the male and female members. Crops include corn, hay, tobacco (which is the chief cash crop, although its use in Amish society is frowned upon), potatoes, beans,

and fruit. Most farms also produce beef, pork, and poultry, and much of the acreage is used to raise feed for the livestock. The Amish at work in their fields with their teams of horses and mules is a scene out of the past and a living testimonial to their religious beliefs. Modern machinery can remove dried corn stalks in the fall and grind them into animal feed within minutes. Yet Amish women and children patiently cut each stalk with a long knife.

Many of the Amish views of farming find reso-

A hitch of six mules is being led along a country road by an Amish farmer. The Amish use draft animals for farm work, and mules are popular with some farmers because of their endurance and the fact that they eat less than horses.

Mules pull a gasoline-powered mower through an Amish tobacco field in Lancaster County, Pa. Population pressures and smaller-sized farms have induced several Amish groups to allow limited modern agricultural technology, such as milking machines and motors on horse-drawn farm implements.

Right: Water wheels provide power for Amish family farms. The sign points to the springhouse, a farm building adjoining a pond or spring and often used for food storage or as a dairy. Crocks and cans are placed in the stream so that they are kept cool.

44

nances in the environmental movement. Implicit in Amish culture is the view that people are the caretakers of God's earth, not exploiters of it. The beauty in the universe is perceived in the orderliness of the seasons, the intricate world of growing plants, the diversity of animals, and the forces of living and dying. People must work in harmony with nature, the soil, and the weather. Farming in a way that causes the soil to lose its fertility is considered sinful and is a charge that can even be brought before the church members, for they believe in the Biblical injunction that "he who robs the soil of its fertility sins against God and man." They must leave the soil to the next generation in as good a condition as when they inherited it. In keeping with this belief,

Amish farmers harvest corn. Because the Amish try to be self-sufficient, they prefer to raise a diversity of crops. However, the steadily diminishing size of their farms has forced them to become more specialized and to raise cash crops.

45

Right: An Amish man drives a wagon loaded with corn. In the 18th century, the Amish depended on wheat as a main source of income, but 200 years later corn is the more profitable crop.

Below: Late summer signals the time for the wheat harvest to these Amish farmers. Pennsylvania has been renowned for the quality of its wheat since the 18th century.

Four young Amish boys bring in a load of tobacco from the fields. Tobacco requires more hand labor than many other crops, but the Amish have the patience and the manpower to grow it successfully. Tobacco is an extremely profitable crop in Lancaster County.

Amish farmers load corn fodder into a horse-drawn baler. After the corn is harvested, the stalks are shredded sometime in November and used as livestock feed.

few Amish farmers would think of using synthetic fertilizers, insecticides, or pesticides. Using organic fertilizer such as manure is considered a superior farming practice because it is a more natural one.

That Lancaster County ranks first in farm income in the United States is due largely to the hard work of the Amish. The rolling pastures where sheep and cattle graze, the fields of tall golden grain, and the long rows of tobacco provide a patchwork of magnificent colors. Every season has farm scenes unequaled in their simple beauty, a reminder of the pre-industrial age when human and animal labor provided the basic necessities of life. And yet, the Amish are able to grow and raise enough food for their families, store adequate provisions until the next harvest, and still have surplus to sell at markets.

COMMUNITY AND ASSISTANCE

The Amish believe in private ownership of property, but the practice of mutual assistance results in what could be called a semicommunal society. Although every Amish farmer operates as a separate economic

Left: An Amish man drives his horses past a neighboring farmer's tractor. Despite their rejection of mechanized farm machinery, the Amish often have their fields plowed and planted before those of conventional farmers.

Below: Riding down a country lane, these Amish pass a bountiful harvest scene in Lancaster County. One reason for such a concentration of Amish in Lancaster County was the Amish preference for its limestone soils, which they believed superior to any other type.

unit, each can always rely on his fellow church members, not only for moral support, but for financial help as well. Since every married Amish man should have his own farm, the community gives him every financial assistance to obtain this goal. If an Amish person needs money to purchase land, family members will loan it at about half the current interest rate charged by a commercial bank. With this ethic of self-help, the Amish discourage any investment from outside the community, and excess earnings are retained for loans to other Amish. Foreclosures are nonexistent, and bank failures or business bankruptcies do not affect them. If, on a

The Sugar Creek Budget.

Vol. 1. SUGAR CREEK, O., MAY 15, 1890. No. 1.

J. C. Miller, Proprietor.
J. M. Richardson, Editor.

TERMS:

50 cts. a year in advance.

THE BUDGET.

In presenting to the public the first issue of the Budget we feel that sense of humility that usually emanates from a knowledge of the criticisms which our little paper and all others of its kind usually meet on being introduced to the reading public.

But dear readers all we ask is that we may meet your recognition

It is not our object to attempt social, political, or religious reforms

It would seem that a new publication brought out without any of these objects was without purpose. Such however is not the case.

Our purpose is to conduct our newspaper in the interest of our village and the vicinity, to give the current news, and to aid in propagating any movement for the general good.

We do not look for our support to sectional jealousies, or contentions between different villages or localities, but desire the patronage of all and distribute all favors equally.

Independent in all things, we maintain the ground of neutrality, and shall fearlessly publish whatever may be of interest and conducive of good morals.

A newspaper in a village, although a small one, is most surely beneficial, and every citizen interested in the prosperity, growth, or business affairs of his place should give it his support.

The Budget will be published regularly Semi-Monthly, and we hope that all who may read this copy have a kindly feeling toward this our first Journalistic enterprise, will make it manifest by sending in their subscriptions, and advertisements.

FINED.

Last Saturday night a young man living a few miles from Shanesville, visited that village, and filled up with tanglefoot. On leaving town he saw fit to break off and destroy several ornamental trees, which Mr. J. H. Wallick had planted along the side walk in front of his residence. Mr. Wallick promptly got out a warrant and had him arrested and brought before Squire Zollars, where he plead guilty, and fine and costs were placed at about Nineteen Dollars.

This affair should teach some people that trees are not planted along the streets to be destroyed.

A great many people are in the habit of using ornamental and shade trees as hitching posts, and thus injuring and destroying them. The law is very strict in such cases. We withold the young man's name, hoping it will be a lesson for him, and that in the future he may not let Benzine and his baser propensities get the better of him

Mr. Moyer, father of our popular station agent, was in town last Tuesday and Wednesday, looking up the interests of the Canton Re pository.

Several very fine large carp have been caught in Sugar Creek this spring. On last Sat. Mr. Levi Hostetler succeeded in landing one which measured 16 in. in length and weighed 2 3-4 lbs. and on the same day Mr. John Deetz captured one which weighed 3 lbs. Two yrs. ago several thousand young carp were placed in the creek by owners of ponds and the result speaks well for the deed.

If you desire to see a fine lot of ladies spring and summer hats call on Mrs. N. C. Beachy. Mrs. B. evinces good taste in the artistic manner in which she trims them.

Miss Mary A. Miller has started a subscription school for primary scholars, and we learn she has secured quite a number of the little folks. Miss Miller is an energetic young woman and parents who have children of the school age should not neglect this chance, as it is much better to have them under the care of a kind and efficient teacher, than to have them running about the streets and sowing the seeds of vice.

Mr. E. Habenstein, of Mt. Hope gave us a look at his smiling countenance a few days ago. We learn he has been employed by N. C. Beachy as an agent for the Solid Comfort Plow.

The man who imagines he is a four horse team with a dog under the wagon sometimes has a bigger load than he can pull,

Get your Job Printing done at the Budget Office.

Page one of the first issue of the *Budget*, the Amish newspaper founded in 1890. This newspaper, which serves Amish and Mennonite communities, is published by a non-Amish press in Ohio.

rare occasion, it is necessary to borrow money from a bank, the loan is underwritten by the church district.

The Amish are aware of one another's needs because most families subscribe to a newspaper called *The Budget*. Published weekly in Sugar Creek, Ohio, by a non-Amish newspaperman, the paper carries news accounts from most Amish settlements throughout North and South America as well as of conservative Mennonite groups. Local contributors from each community provide accounts of births, marriages, deaths, accidents, and of any unusual happenings. Health matters, with weekly progress reports concerning the chronically ill, as well as farm sales, moves, and other local news appear in this newspaper. Occasionally, *The Budget* asks for financial assistance for an unfortunate Amish family, and it is not unusual for contributions to come from Amish communities throughout both continents.

An Amish farmer in Lancaster County transfers his tobacco harvest from the field to his shed where it will hang to cure. More than 10,000 acres of cigar tobacco are grown in the county, much of it by the Amish.

Scores of Amish farmers assemble to raise a new barn for another Amish family near Leola in Lancaster County. During the all-day barn raising, the women cook and provide meals and refreshments for the men.

All forms of government farm subsidies and disaster aid are refused. Since the Amish do not believe in commercial insurance on their property, local agreements call for community sharing of damages. If, for example, a member's barn is destroyed by fire, the community will rebuild it. Usually the farmer who suffers a loss due to fire or windstorm will pay one-fourth of the cost himself and the remaining three-fourths is divided among the community members. (Amish barns have no lightning rods because that, they believe, would be tampering with God's will.) About 200 Amish men can work all day "barn raising" without any financial return, and the women provide the noontime meal. Similarly, if a member is ill or incapacitated, the community will plow, seed, or harvest his fields. Faith and fellowship truly dominate every aspect of Amish life.

Working together is a mainstay of Amish life. Here neighbors gather for a barn raising. This task is usually finished in one day and is done in the spirit of cooperation—there is no monetary payment.

Three children walk home from school on a scenic country road near Intercourse, Pa. The ungraded classrooms promote a sense of community among Amish schoolchildren, a quality that lasts throughout adulthood.

"Rent a farm, milk cows, learn a trade, if possible, do manual labor as did Paul, and all that which you then fall short of will doubtlessly be given and provided you by pious brethren."
The words of Menno Simons, written in the 16th century, hold true for the Amish today.

CHAPTER FOUR

EDUCATION

One of the most crucial issues facing the Amish in the 20th century has been the preservation of their way of life against the inroads of modern civilization. This dilemma has been most acute in the area of education; here the right of the Amish to practice their religious beliefs undisturbed runs head-on against laws concerning compulsory education, a fundamental doctrine of democratic society.

Tree of Life, Ohio

Although the Bill of Rights does not guarantee free, compulsory education, it had been assumed since the founding of the United States that popular government requires a literate public. But it was not until the 1890s that most states adopted compulsory school attendance laws. Progressive educators, prompted by a desire to "Americanize" the large number of immigrants pouring into the country, pressed for more aggressive enforcement of education laws. Several court cases upheld the concept of compulsory schooling on the grounds that it was essential for the "welfare of the minor" and that education safeguards the welfare of the community and the safety of the state.

The Amish are not against education but they are opposed to modern schools that teach more than the basic skills of reading, writing, and arithmetic. They see compulsory education as a force leading to assimilation with the outside world, and public schools are perceived as a serious threat to their homogeneity. The Amish oppose school busing and the use of audiovisual materials, as well as curriculums that include courses in career goals, athletics, music, the teaching of evolution, and the use of science laboratories. They also resist tenure for teachers, since God intended that the ill-prepared or poor teacher do some other kind of work. The Amish feel that education should prepare one

Father and son drive past a one-room school in Lancaster County. Although at home the Amish speak Pennsylvania Dutch, at school these children learn English.

Rows of old-fashioned desks await installation in an Amish schoolhouse in Lancaster County. One-room schools in the Old Order Amish parochial system provide students with a formal education through the eighth grade, after which children leave to help their parents full-time on the farm.

for farm work or the ministry, and both vocations can best be learned from the family.

Thus, the Amish feel that not only is high school irrelevant for them, but that by exposing their children to worldly values their chance of eternal salvation could be impaired. Although the Amish gradually established their own parochial schools, this did not solve the problem regarding state compulsory attendance laws—in most states, the minimum age for leaving school requires attendance at a high school for one or more years, and high schools are required to offer a certain number of courses in science, physical education, and other subjects opposed by the Amish. The Amish resisted sending their children to high school, parochial or other, and thereby set the stage for a dramatic court case involving the rights of a religious minority when in conflict with state education laws.

CONFLICT WITH SECULARISM

After being sentenced to five days in jail for refusing to pay fines for not sending their children to high school, these Amish elders in Honey Brook, Pa., gathered to discuss strategy in 1960. They had refused to enroll their children because they considered the school "too worldly."

The case concerned the small Amish community of Green County, Wisconsin. The Amish first arrived in Green County in 1963. By 1968, there were 24 Amish families in the community. They had come searching for less expensive agricultural land. Sky-rocketing real estate values in Pennsylvania had made farming, particularly for young families, increasingly difficult.

From the time of their arrival, the Amish clashed with school authorities. One parent objected, for example, to his daughter's attendance in a high school physical education class because she would be forced to wear shorts. Another opposed the teaching of evolution in the required science textbook. In 1968, public school authorities of Green County insisted that the small Amish community send their children to the local high school. The Amish refused, defying a Wisconsin state law requiring school attendance until the age of 16. The

A classroom in a New Order Amish parochial school in Kinsman, Ohio. Compared to the Old Order, New Order Amish are considered more liberal in religious doctrine, even permitting some use of telephones, electricity, and tractors.

lower court upheld the school authorities. The case was eventually appealed to the Wisconsin Supreme Court, which ruled that enforced schooling of Amish children beyond the eighth grade was a violation of the free exercise of the religious rights of the Amish—a decision upheld by the Supreme Court of the United States.

In the landmark 1972 Supreme Court decision (*Wisconsin* v. *Yoder*), the Court voted unanimously to exempt the Amish from state compulsory attendance laws beyond the elementary grades. "It is neither fair nor correct to suggest that the Amish are opposed to education beyond the eighth-grade level," wrote Chief Justice Warren Burger. "What the record shows is that they are opposed to conventional formal education of the type provided by a certified high school because it comes at the child's crucial adolescent period of religious development." The Court ruled that the Amish did not pose

Barefoot Amish youngsters walk to their one-room school in Leacock, Pa. Amish schools have had trouble finding textbooks considered acceptable by the church elders. The Old Order Book Society prints many of the books used by Amish children.

a threat to public safety, but that forcing them to attend high school would violate their religious rights.

Today, Amish children attend local parochial one-room schoolhouses, which are ungraded. They do not attend high school. Amish families pay both the required local school taxes and support their own school system.

Although they recognize that formal education is useful, the Amish believe that the family is the best teacher. At school, an Amish child can learn the three R's with his brothers, sisters, cousins, and friends, but the real education takes place in the home. Girls are taught to sew, cook, and bake. Boys learn carpentry and, above all, the skills of farming. These fundamentals cannot be learned in a schoolroom but must be learned by actual experience. Both boys and girls tend to farm chores, take care of animals, and help their parents in any way they can.

THE SCHOOL DAY

All Amish schools follow the same basic schedule, which is not much different from the traditional rural schoolhouses at the turn of the 20th century. The day is divided into four periods of approximately one-and-one-half hours each. There is a recess between each period and a lunch break at noon. All schools begin the day with hymn singing in both English and German. Then there is a reading from the Bible. The children learn English (reading, grammar, spelling, penmanship, and composition) and arithmetic (addition, subtraction, multiplication, long division, percentages, ratios, and simple and compound interest). The techniques of New Math are not taught. Textbooks are quite old-fashioned

Laughing Amish schoolgirls enjoy recess in Leacock, Pa. As the number of Amish schools has increased, the Amish have provided teachers, usually single women, from their own community.

by today's public-school standards. Some Amish schools use reprints of the original 19th-century *McGuffey Reader*, but even here, some of the stories are considered too patriotic and militaristic. Amish schools avoid fairy tales, myths, or stories in which animals talk, and anything dealing with sex. Every story must have a moral. When history is taught, the emphasis is on Amish history, but children are taught the basic facts of American history, especially about the constitutional guarantees of religious freedom, and how the authors of the Constitution opened each session with a prayer.

The Amish fear assimilation into American culture. Therefore, in addition to the basic subjects most Amish elementary schools teach German. As John Hostetler and Gertrude Huntington explain in

Children in Amish Society (1971): The relationship between English (the language of the world), German (the language of the Bible), and Pennsylvania Dutch (the language of the home) is a subject of concern in many Amish communities. Pennsylvania Dutch is the preferred spoken language and is used exclusively within the household and community; it is the family's responsibility to give its children a firm foundation in the mother tongue. In addition, the children must learn to speak, read, and write English to live successfully on the margin of the twentieth century; it is the responsibility of the school to teach the children English. So, an Amish child must be able to read the Bible in German, speak the Pennsylvania Dutch dialect, and understand English.

In essence the controversy between the Amish and secular officials over education—whether it be

A group of young Amish men engage in a game of corner, or mush, ball, a favorite sport, as the girls watch. It is a rough sport. Players in each corner of a square try to hit their opponents in the center with a hide-covered ball of straw.

over curriculum, teacher training and certification, or state attendance laws—has to do with the simple fact that the American education system perpetuates certain social values that it feels represent the majority. The Amish, on the other hand, are concerned with maintaining their status as a minority and keeping their distinctive beliefs from being overwhelmed by the surrounding culture.

A young Amish boy follows his father's mule-drawn grain drill during spring planting. Similar methods are used by Amish farmers to till a quarter of Lancaster County's 336,150 field acres.

Laughing and jostling, these Amish boys enter their one-room schoolhouse after recess. With children of different ages and levels in one classroom, the teacher must spend part of each day concentrating on each age group.

Despite modern styles, beach wear for the Amish shows how intent they are in retaining their deep-seated traditional way of life.

CHAPTER FIVE

THE AMISH TODAY

Studies of Amish society show that their communities suffer from the same problems as the outside society—alcoholism, juvenile delinquency, emotional problems such as anxiety and stress, and suicide. Whenever possible, the Amish community attempts to handle the problem itself.

The Amish believe that the technological progress of the 20th century has increased the temptations of the world. Therefore, they must withdraw even further from the evils that surround them. Those who cannot continue in the traditions of their forefathers, perhaps 10% to 15% of the community, usually join conservative Mennonite churches, which is rather a halfway compromise between Amish austerity and modern secularism. Nevertheless, the Amish, because of their high birthrate and close-knit society, are increasing in numbers.

Bow Tie, Ohio

HEALTH

The cultural and physical isolation of the Amish has affected their overall health patterns. Although the infant mortality rate is slightly higher for the Amish than the national average (possibly as a result of infant deaths from birth defects), on the whole the Amish tend to live longer than the general population. The number of deaths from cancer, heart disease, and circulatory, respiratory, and digestive ailments is much lower among the Amish than it is for the non-Amish population. Possible reasons are the comparative simplicity of farm life and the vigorous exercise this entails. The fact that the food of the Amish is organically grown, with no preservatives or additives, and that there is generally lower pollution in the country than found in city or in-

About one-half of the Amish population in the United States accepted vaccination against polio after the dreaded disease had crippled a number of Amish during an outbreak among them in 1979.

Joe King, an Amish man from Lancaster County, studies his portrait at a Lancaster art show. He is something of an exception among his peers since most Amish consider it vain to pose for paintings or photos.

dustrial environments, probably contributes to the higher-than-average longevity that the Amish enjoy.

The principles and tenets of Jakob Ammann and his original followers have been faithfully maintained by his disciples for almost 300 years. Despite their forced migration to the New World and despite the mores and cultures of the peoples surrounding them, this group has resolutely clung to its literal interpretation of the Scriptures and to the values of its founder.

The Amish have tried to keep the distinction between their community and the rest of American society. They refuse to fight in wars or take oaths, and do not run for public office, although they do register to vote and will vote in large numbers on issues that involve them personally, for example, to elect a school superintendent or on other local issues. Seldom do they vote in state and national elections. They ignore national holidays and birthdays of heroes, as any form of nationalism, they believe, is contrary to religious principle. Their holidays are religious ones, and on these no work is done. Twice a year, on Good Friday and in early October, they have fast days, that is, they eat no breakfast—a tremendous sacrifice for the hardworking Amish. Easter Sunday, Easter Monday, and Ascension Day are days of celebration. Thanksgiving is generally observed, as it is a religious as well as a national holiday. New Year's Day is another Amish holiday. But that is all. Even Christmas, a joyous time, is kept as simple as possible. In keeping with the austere traditions of the Amish, there are no trees, no holly wreaths, and no colored lights.

An Amish carriage being outfitted with blinking electric warning lights on its rear to comply with Pennsylvania state law. The carriage shop, owned by John Lapp, specializes in making the lights that are placed on the shafts of the vehicles.

THE AMISH AND
THE OUTSIDE WORLD

The picturesque village of Intercourse, Pa., with Amish buggies lined up at a hitching post. Amish communities provide for themselves and others many services and tools made obsolete by modern American technology. Thus Amish insure their self-sufficiency in all their needs.

There is, however, a nagging problem for these ascetic, pious people—criticism by outsiders. While tourists snap photos of the lovely farms of Lancaster County and return home with glowing accounts of the enchanting Plain People, some neighbors of the Amish, albeit a minority, are critical and resentful. Some covet the prime Amish farmland in Lancaster County, which is passed from one generation to the next, and thus unavailable for purchase by outsiders. Some neighbors are irritated by the disruption of

An Amish schoolgirl takes a swing during a softball game near Kinsman, Ohio. Amish families in this community built their own schoolhouse for their children.

privacy caused by the millions of tourists. Others believe the Amish receive special treatment, since the Amish do not serve in the armed forces, do not pay Social Security taxes, and their children are exempt from attending high school. Although the Amish lead a humble life, they have, through the value of their farmlands, accumulated considerable wealth, yet they take the position that wealth is the unholy temptation of a worldly society.

Some indications of outside resentment can be seen by scanning the letters to the editor of a local Lancaster newspaper. For example, in 1984 when a five-year-old Amish youth died in a farm accident, numerous letters blasted the Amish practice of allowing children to work farm equipment. One writer suggested that the youth's parents be charged with neglect and abuse. There have also been letters criticizing the horse-drawn buggies of the Amish,

Young Amish schoolchildren have to face the complex pressures of modern society while maintaining and continuing the Amish way of life.

An Amish farmer. In Europe the Amish were famous for restoring fertility to soil depleted by poor farming methods. Their procedures included crop rotation, irrigation, use of natural fertilizers such as manure, and the raising of clover and alfalfa to replenish the soil.

claiming that the steel horseshoes tear up the road, and other letters have charged that the Amish receive preferential treatment from the police.

In general, however, the two distinct societies—one worldly and the other ascetic—exist in relative harmony. Because of the Amish population's long existence in Lancaster County, most residents seem to be comfortable with their neighbors.

The Amish are united by their families, faith, and traditions. This must be the reason that the fellowship has endured for so long. Austere as they may be, their lives are full of joy and happiness. They are indeed a people apart and yet a people together.

FURTHER READING

Horst, Mel, and Smith, Elmer. *The Amish*. Whitmore, Pa.: Applied Arts, 1966.

Horst, Mel, and Smith, Elmer. *Among the Amish*. Allentown, Pa.: Pennsylvania German Folklore Society, 1959.

Hostetler, John. *Amish Life*. Scottsdale, Pa.: Herald Press, 1983.

Hostetler, John. *Amish Society*. Baltimore: Johns Hopkins University Press, 1963, 3rd ed. 1983.

Hostetler, John, and Huntington, Gertrude. *Children in Amish Society*. New York: Exposition Press, 1971.

Jordan, Mildred. *The Distelfink Country of the Pennsylvania Dutch*. New York: Crown Publishers, Inc., 1978

Rice, Charles, and Steinmetz, Rollin. *The Amish Year*. New Brunswick: Rutgers University Press, 1956.

Smith, C. Henry, *The Mennonite Immigration to Pennsylvania*. Norristown, Pa.: Pennsylvania German Society, 1929.

Smith, Elmer. *The Amish Today*. Norristown, Pa.: Pennsylvania German Society, 1961.

Warner, James, and Denlinger, Donald. *The Gentle People*. New York: Grossman Publications, 1969.

Wood, Ralph, ed. *The Pennsylvania Germans*. Princeton: Princeton University Press, 1942.

INDEX

a

alcoholism, 69
Ammann, Jakob
    as Amish founder, 15
    communion frequency, idea of, 17
    dress uniformity and, 17
    footwashing and, 17
    hairstyle uniformity and, 17
    view of shunning, 16, 17
Anabaptists
    persecution of, 14
    split from Zwingli, 14
    see also Mennonites
animals
    use of, 43
Ascension Day, 71
assimilation
    fear of, 58, 61, 64, 65
assistance
    belief in, 48
auctions
    as social events, 41
Ausbund, 29
automobiles
    ban on, 3
Aylmer, Ontario, 41

b

baptism
    age level for, 32
    choice of, 41
    instruction, 32
barn raising, 54, 55
Belgian horse, 7
Berks County, Pennsylvania
    as Amish center, 1
Bible
    basis for Protestant revolt, 12, 13
    as core of Amish life, 1, 17, 25
    footwashing, 17
    Mennonite literalness of
      interpretation, 14
birth control
    prohibition on, 5
birthrate, 5
bishop
    functions, 26
bridge, covered, 23
Budget, The, 50, 51
buggy
    styles, 3
    traffic signs on, 26
    use of, 6, 33
    warning lights on, 72
Burger, Warren, 61
burial rites, 35

c

Canada
    Amish migration to, 3, 21–23
cemetery, 35
children, 56, 75
    behavior of, 24
    clothing of, 3
    discipline, 24
    as home helpers, 63
    relationships with, 36
Children in Amish Society, 65
Christmas, 72
church
    membership, basis of, 25
    religious hierarchy, 25, 26
    selection of officials, 28
    Sunday meetings, 25
church and state, 14
cities
    attitudes toward, 41
clothing
    making, 38
    marriage dress, 32
    men's, 2
    styles, 1
    winter, 3
    women's, 2
Coligny, Admiral, 10
commercialization, 6
communion
    description of, 31
    frequency of, 17
community
    sense of, 48
compulsory education laws, 58, 59
    Amish exemption from high
      school, 61
    Amish resistance to, 57
consubstantiation, 13
Continental Congress, 21
corn
    as cash crop, 45, 46
    use of, 48
corner (mush) ball, 65
covered bridge, 23
cuisine, 39
curriculum, school, 63

d

deacon
    functions of, 26
death
    customs, 35
decor, home, 37
Delaware, 20
Disciples of Christ, 20

divorce
    ban on, 34
dress, 17
Dubois, François, 10
Dunkers
    practices of, 20

e

Easter, 71
ecology
    concern with, 45
education, 57–67
    controversy over, 60, 65
    in the home, 63
    laws, conflict with, 59
    length of, 56
    and religious freedom, 60
    role, of, 57, 58
    see also compulsory education laws
elderly
    Amish care of, 39
electricity
    ban on, 3, 39
Elmira, Ontario
    as Amish center, 22
embalming, 35
endogamy
    practice of, 4
English language, 59, 65
environment
    Amish philosophy of, 43, 76
Essex County, Ontario, 21
Eucharist
    Catholic-Protestant differences, 13
excommunication, 16
extended family, 38

f

family
    extended, 38
    importance of, 5
    Mennonite, 15
    structure, 5
farming
    efficiency, 49
    equipment, 18, 44
    income, levels of, 42, 48
    life, 37
    as main occupation, 41
    methods, 66
    practices, 18
    products, 42
    and religion, 41, 43
    tobacco, 52
fast days, 71
food, 39

footwashing
    description of, 31
    Ammann and, 17
Fraktur
    calligraphy, 14
    typeface, 27
France
    religious wars, 10
freedom of religion
    education and, 60
    migration from Europe, 18
Froschauer, Christopher, 16
fruit pies, 39
funeral rites, 35
furniture, 38

g

games, 65
genetics
    problems of inbreeding, 5
German language
    speech dialect, 2
    teaching of, 64
    use of high German, 31
Germantown, Pennsylvania
    first Mennonite settlement, 18
Germany, 3, 11
Good Friday
    fasting, 71
government aid
    acceptance of, 39
    refusal of, 54
Grebel, Konrad
    religious revolt of, 13
Green County, Wisconsin
    education controversy, 60

h

hairstyle
    Ammann and rules on, 17
    regulation of, 2
hats, 30
headcovering, women's, 3
health
    concerns, 70
hierarchy, religious, 26
High German
    hymns in, 29
    use of, 29
high school
    exemption from, 61
    resistance to, 59, 60
    Supreme Court case, 60
Holbein, Hans, the Younger, 11
holidays, 71
holy kiss, 31

home
    decor, 37
    as educational center, 63
    life, 37
    multigenerational, 38
horse
    and buggy, 3
    Belgian draft, 7
Hostetler, John, 64
Huguenots
    Catholic slaughter of, 10
Huntington Gertrude, 61
hymn
    singing, 29
    themes of, 29
"Hymn of Praise," 29
hymnal, Amish: see *Ausbund*

i

Illinois, 20
immunization, 70
inbreeding
    and genetic problems, 5
income
    corn as cash crop, 45, 46
    farming, 42
    tobacco as cash crop, 45, 52
Indiana, 4
indulgence, 11
infant mortality, 5, 70
insurance
    lack of, 54
intermarriage
    prevalence of, 5
Iowa, 20

j

jewelry
    avoidance of, 3

k

Kapp, 30
Kent County, Ontario, 21
kiss, holy, 31
kitchen
    as center of home, 39

l

Lancaster County, Pennsylvania
    as Amish center, 1, 4
    countryside, 37
    farm income, 48
    limestone soil of, 49
    as tobacco-growing center, 47, 52
    tourism, 5
life span, 70
lifestyle
    Biblical importance in, 1

    Mennonite-Amish differences on, 18
lighting, home, 39
limestone soil, 21, 49
love feast, 20
Luther, Martin
    Protestant Revolt and, 11
    Zwingli, conflict with, 12, 13
Lutheran Church
    founding of, 13

m

machinery
    avoidance of modern, 43
marriage
    customs, 33, 34
Martyr's Mirror, The
    as persecution record, 14
Maryland, 20
McGuffey Reader, 63
medical services, 39
meetings, Sunday, 28–31
Meidung (shunning), 16, 17
membership, church
    age for, 14
    basis of, 25
    districts, 25
    growth, 4
    see also population
men
    beards and moustaches, 2
    clothing of, 2
    division of labor, 38
    separation from women at
     meetings, 28
Menno Simons, 14
Mennonites
    Amish, split from, 15
    Amish lifestyle, differences from, 18
    flight from Europe, 14, 15
    literal Biblical interpretation, 14
    settlement in America, 17, 18
    see also Anabaptists
milk, 42
minister
    functions of, 26
mule
    as farm animal, 37
mush (corner) ball, 65

n

New Order Amish
    practices of, 61
New Year's Day, 72
newspaper
    role of, 51

o

officials, church
  backgrounds of, 26
  selection of, 28
Ohio
  as Amish center, 4, 20
Old Order Amish, 61
Old Order Book Society
  as textbook publisher, 62
Ontario
  Amish in, 3, 22

p

parochial school, 59, 63
penance, 11
Penn, William
  religious freedom and, 18, 19
Pennsylvania
  as Amish center, 3, 20
  religious denominations in, 19
  religious freedom in, 15, 18–20
Pennsylvania Dutch
  commercialization of area, 6
  dialect, 2
  language, importance of, 64
  language, use of, 58
persecution, religious
  of Amish, 14
  Mennonite migration from
    Europe, 18
pie
  fruit, 39
  shoo-fly, 40
polio, 70
pollution, 70
population
  background, 3
  growth, 3, 5, 69
  locations, 3, 4
  numbers, 3
  see also membership, church
practices, Amish, 25
preserves, 40
property, 48
Protestant Reformation
  effects of, 9, 10
  Martin Luther and, 11
Protestantism
  divisions in, 13
Pyle, Howard, 20

q

quilt, 38

r

Reformed Church
  founding of, 13
religion, Amish, 25–35

centrality to Amish of, 25
farming methods and, 41, 43
freedom in the New World, 15
hierarchy, 26
history, 9
meeting places, 25
split with Mennonites, 15
views on education, 60
remarriage, 35
Revolutionary War, U.S., 21
Roman Catholicism, 10, 11
  Eucharist, 13

s

St. Bartholomew's Day massacre, 10
Sandy Foundation, The, 19
school
  curriculum, 63
  parochial, 59, 63
sermon, 29
Sermon on the Mount, 14
Seventh-Day Adventists, 20
shaving
  customs, 2
shoo-fly pie
  recipe, 40
shunning (Meidung), 16, 17
Simons, Menno, 14
singings
  as social events, 41
sleigh
  as winter transportation, 22
social life, Amish, 30, 41
soil
  care of, 45
  conservation practices, 76
  of Lancaster County, 49
souvenirs, 6
speech, 2
sports, 65
springhouse, 44
state education laws
  conflict with, 59
Sugar Creek, Ohio, 51
Sunday
  meal, pattern of, 31
  meetings, 28–31
  services, frequency of, 25
  services, order of, 30
Supreme Court, U.S., 61, 63
Swiss Brethren: see Anabaptists;
  Mennonites
Switzerland, 3, 12

t

taxes
  payment of, 39
teachers, 64

ideas about, 58
technology
  use of, 44
teenagers
  activities of, 41
textbooks, 63
  standards of, 62
Thanksgiving, 71, 72
three-generation house, 38
tobacco
  as cash crop, 43, 46, 47, 52
tradition
  importance of, 9
tourism
  as major industry, 5, 6
  problems created by, 73
tractor, 18
transportation, 19
  sleigh in winter, 22
transubstantiation, 13

u

United Brethren, 20
uppingblock
  use of, 33

v

vanity
  avoidance of, 3
visiting
  as main social activity, 40

w

walnut tree, 21
water wheel
  as power source, 44
Waterloo County, Ontario, 22
wedding
  as social affair, 32
wheat, 42, 46, 51
widowhood, 35
windmill, 38
winter
  clothing, 3
  transportation, 22
Wisconsin
  migration to, 60
Wisconsin v. Yoder, 61
Witness, 6
women
  clothing of, 2, 30
  home crafts and, 38

z

Zurich, Switzerland, 12
Zwingli, Huldreich
  as anti-Catholic, 12
  Martin Luther, conflict with, 13
  persecution of Mennonites, 14
  reforms of, 12